CUPIDS

CUPIDS

LINDSAY PORTER

PHOTOGRAPHS BY GLORIA NICOL

LORENZ BOOKS

LONDON • NEW YORK • SYDNEY • BATH

First published in 1996 by Lorenz Books

© 1996 Anness Publishing Limited

Lorenz Books is an imprint of
Anness Publishing Limited
Boundary Row Studios
1 Boundary Row
London SE1 8HP

This edition is distributed in Canada by
Raincoast Books Distribution Limited

ISBN 1 85967 267 1

Publisher: Joanna Lorenz
Copy Editor: Deborah Savage
Designer: Lilian Lindblom
Step photographer: Lucy Tizard
Illustrator: Lucinda Ganderton
Introduction by Beverley Jollinson

Printed in Singapore by
Star Standard Industries Pte Ltd

CONTENTS

INTRODUCTION 6

NURSERY CUSHION WITH MUSICAL CUPID 12

WINGED CUPID BROOCH 14

COPPER CUPID MOBILE 16

MAJOLICA-STYLE TILES 20

GINGERBREAD CUPIDS 22

GILDED FILIGREE LAMPSHADE 24

CRACKLE-GLAZED "ANTIQUE" PRINT 27

CONTEMPLATIVE CUPID CARD 29

FROSTED GLASS JUG 32

LOVE-TOKEN BOWL 34

GILDED CUPID BORDER 36

BAROQUE VELVET CUSHION 40

CUPID WRAPPING PAPER 42

CUPID CAMISOLE 44

CUPID DRESSING-TABLE MIRROR 46

FOLK-ART STYLE HAND-PAINTED BOX 50

CUPID LINOCUT 52

WINGS OF LOVE WALL DECORATION 54

"IVORY" CUPID 56

GOLD AND SILVER VALENTINE'S CARD 58

TEMPLATES 60

ACKNOWLEDGEMENTS 64

INTRODUCTION

The little god of love with his golden bow and arrow, cheeky, chubby and aged about three, seems pretty harmless and sweet these days. He's a jokey little figure who goes with hearts and flowers and decorates millions of Valentines every February. He wasn't always so inoffensive; the truth is, poor Cupid has come down in the world.

His name means desire; he was one of many deities adopted by the Romans from the Greeks, who called him Eros and for whom he represented erotic love. He began life as a very powerful god indeed. In fact, the earliest myths about Eros suggest that it was he who brought about the union of Gaia and Uranus, the earth and sky, and presided over the creation of gods and men.

Then along came love. The romantic ideas of the Greeks gave rise to a new version of Eros as the child of Aphrodite, the goddess of love, and Ares, the god of war. The union of these two underlined the fact that it was often love that began the conflict, as in the case of the Trojan War, and the mischievous Eros (or Cupid) could be relied upon to stir up everyone's passions. From now on he was portrayed as a child who was as irrational as love itself.

Cupid is armed with a bow and arrows. He has two sorts of arrow in his quiver: those that are gold inspire love, but others are tipped with lead and anyone hit by one of these will remain stony-hearted. This gives him plenty of scope for making trouble. He's often shown wearing a blindfold: he stands for blind love, but it also means his arrows can land anywhere and no one is safe. Sometimes he carries a torch, representing the flames of passion, but his arrows are the dominant image. A heart transfixed by an arrow is universal shorthand for the helpless state of being in love – a simple symbol to be carved on a tree or drawn in an anonymous Valentine message.

Top: Classic Victorian Valentine with sentimental cupid figures.

We often think of cupids in the plural, and this isn't just a decorative device: it started with the Greeks and Romans. Called erotes or cupidines, they reflected the many different facets of love. From them derived the winged babies known as *putti*. These little guardian spirits were often carved on sarcophagi and when the artists of the Renaissance began to take their inspiration from the surviving sculpture of the Graeco-Roman world, they adopted the *putti* enthusiastically.

Cupid appears in Renaissance paintings with all his classical attributes. In Botticelli's *Primavera* he is hovering above the figure of Venus poised to shoot, a chubby baby in a blindfold. Raphael's *Galatea* is even less fortunate and beset by three cupids aiming at her simultaneously, while a fourth, equipped with spare arrows, hides scowling behind a cloud.

Left: Terracotta relief depicting a bacchante and infant satyr. This little figure is a close relation of the Graeco-Roman cupidines.

During the Baroque period, cupid figures managed to escape from mythological scenes into contemporary life. They are out in force in Rubens' *Garden of Love*, overseeing the dalliance of seventeenth-century couples in a country garden. A century later, they're still hovering over contemporary lovers in the paintings of Watteau. Even the cool, dispassionate Vermeer uses Cupid's symbolic power. In his painting of a girl reading a letter, he makes it clear that it is a love letter by placing a picture of Cupid on the wall behind her.

Above: Sixteenth-century ink and chalk studies of putti, *by Giovanni Baglione. This subject was very popular during the Renaissance, due to a renewed interest in the art of the Classical world.*

Left: By the Victorian age, Cupid had been transformed into a harmless figure of romance.

In the theatrical splendour of Italian Baroque decoration, cupids flourished in carved and gilded ornaments and ornate plasterwork and fluttered amongst the rosy clouds of Tiepolo's ceilings. This is the style in which we most enjoy them now, using plaster mouldings, gilding and luxurious textiles to recreate the Baroque spirit of opulent excess.

When the first-century ruins of Pompeii and Herculanaeum were unearthed in the 1740s, masses of cupids were discovered painted on the walls of the houses. In the borders below large panels depicting serious heroic or religious subjects a riot of the little fellows busied themselves, played games, rode on crabs, or drove coaches pulled by swans or dolphins. They were painted in a free and airy style and were instantly taken up by eighteenth-century designers. The little pictures were much copied in neoclassical interiors.

Above: Detail of Swedish-empire style ceramic tiled stove, at Tido Castle, Vasteras.

Right: Detail of Roman fresco from Pompeii.

As decorative motifs, especially in bedrooms, the popularity of cupids was assured because of what they represented. They appeared as porcelain figures, as ornaments on clocks, or on carved mirrors. Even austere Empire-style designs included cupids, although they were more likely to be virile-looking figures cast in bronze. A winged figure armed with a bow was to become so closely identified with

passionate love that when a statue called *The Spirit of Christian Charity* was erected in central London the general public instantly renamed it Eros.

While the Gothic revival, combined with the prudery of nineteenth-century Britain and America, diminished the acceptability of cupids in the bedroom, another vogue kept them in the public eye. Valentine cards began to be printed early in the century, and were fantastically popular. The market was very competitive and all sorts of ingenious designs, involving lace, paper, ribbons and mirrors, pop-up bouquets and secret messages, were devised. Cupids naturally loomed large in these fantastic concoctions, but they were of the sentimental, harmless variety which still endures to this day. Cupid certainly has evolved over the centuries, and these days

Above: Raphael's Galatea *is beset on all sides by mischievous cupids.*

Left: Detail from Bottecelli's Primavera, *with the traditional depiction of blind Cupid.*

going over the top is perhaps what Cupid is best at. However, a light-hearted flurry of hearts, flowers and gilded wings is sure to be welcomed by nearly everyone. If you're in love, or just thinking about it, have fun with the ideas in this book.

NURSERY CUSHION WITH MUSICAL CUPID

This is a delightful cushion that would lend a touch of jollity to any nursery and would also make a lovely accessory for a bedroom chair.

YOU WILL NEED

MATERIALS
42 cm/16½ in square white
  sprigged cotton fabric
3 skeins dark red stranded
  embroidery thread
4 strips darker patterned
  cotton fabric, 1 m x 14 cm/
  1 yd x 5½ in
matching and contrasting
  sewing threads
2 rectangles plain cotton fabric,
  30 x 42 cm/12 x 16½ in
120 cm/48 in dark red velvet
  ribbon, 1.5 cm/½ in wide
40 cm/16 in square cushion pad

EQUIPMENT
dressmaker's carbon paper
embroidery hoop
needle
sewing machine
dressmaker's pins

1 Enlarge the template from the back of the book. Transfer to the sprigged fabric, with dressmaker's carbon paper. Stretch the fabric in an embroidery hoop. Embroider the outline in chain-stitch. To make the frill, join the darker cotton fabric strips together and hem one long edge.

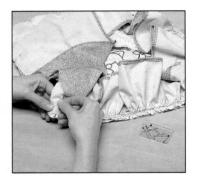

2 Run a gathering thread along the edge opposite the hem. With right sides together, pin the gathers to the embroidered cushion front, matching the four joins to the four corners. Draw up the gathering thread until the frill fits the cushion, pin and stitch.

3 For the backing, stitch a double hem along one long side of each rectangle of plain fabric. With right sides together, place one rectangle at each end of the embroidered front, so that the hemmed edges lie to the centre. Pin and stitch round the outer edge, leaving a small seam allowance. Turn the cushion the right way out. Make four bows from the velvet ribbon. Sew to the corners of the cushion. Insert the pad.

WINGED CUPID BROOCH

This exotic piece of jewellery is made from papier-mâché pulp, hand-painted in gorgeous colours and then decorated with artificial gemstones and glass tear-drops.

YOU WILL NEED

MATERIALS
thin card
papier-mâché pulp
wallpaper paste
newspaper
PVA glue
white acrylic primer
flat-backed glass gems
epoxy resin glue
eye-hook pins
selection of gouache paints
clear matt varnish
gold enamel paint
small glass tear-drop beads
small jump-rings
brooch fixing

EQUIPMENT
pencil
craft knife
self-healing cutting mat
medium and fine paintbrushes
dressmaker's pin
paint-mixing container
round-nosed pliers

1 Trace the template from the back of the book on to the card and cut it out with the craft knife. Cover with papier-mâché pulp and then apply several layers of wallpaper paste and newspaper strips. Allow to dry.

2 Coat with PVA glue and then white primer. Leave to dry between each stage. Glue the glass gems with epoxy resin. Make holes with a pin and insert the eye-hook pins, securing them with epoxy resin.

3 Paint on your design with gouache paints. When dry, coat with matt varnish. Leave to dry again, then add gold enamel details.

4 Assemble all the brooch pieces and tear-drops beads, joining them with jump-rings, using the pliers. Glue the brooch fixing into position.

COPPER CUPID MOBILE

The glowing warmth of copper catches the light very gracefully as the mobile moves. The mobile looks spectacular and yet is easily worked in wire and thin sheet metal. To help you form the cupid figure, try drawing it out on paper first and then use your drawing as a guide for bending the wires.

YOU WILL NEED

MATERIALS
15 x 4 cm/6 x 1½ in thin copper sheet
3 m/3 yd thin copper wire
1 m/1 yd medium copper wire
1 m/1 yd fine gold-coloured wire
epoxy resin glue

EQUIPMENT
pencil
scrap paper
scissors
tin snips
wet and dry sandpaper
hammer and nail
round-nosed pliers

1 Draw a heart and arrow freehand on scrap paper and cut them out. Trace three hearts and one arrow head and flight on to the copper sheet.

2 Cut the shapes out with tin snips and sand the edges smooth to the touch with wet and dry sandpaper.

3 Pierce holes in the hearts, by hammering a nail through the metal.

4 Use the pliers to bend a cupid shape from the thin copper wire. In this design the cupid is made in two sections: the head, torso and arm are made from one length of wire, and the legs from another. Bend the medium copper wire into a bow shape.

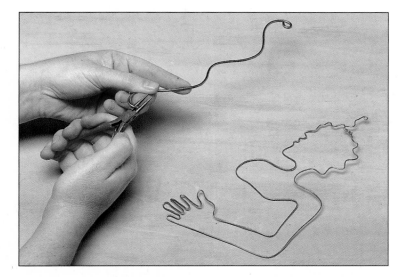

5 Attach the two parts of the cupid with short lengths of thin wire.

6 Bend three heart shapes from the thin copper wire. Attach the copper hearts to the inside of the wire hearts with lengths of gold-coloured wire.

7 Bend the arrow head to make a groove in which the shaft will lie. Do the same with the flight. Cut a 15 cm/6 in length of medium wire for the shaft and glue it in place.

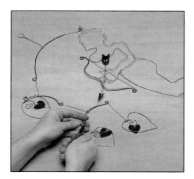

8 Use gold-coloured wire to create the string of the bow and connect it to the bow. Insert the arrow between the cupid's fingers and connect the bow to the cupid's chest. Cut two 12 cm/4¾ in lengths of medium wire and one 25 cm/10 in length for the struts. Bend the ends into loops. Assemble the mobile pieces using the gold-coloured wire.

Majolica-style Tiles

Majolica is glazed or enamelled earthenware, noted for its bright colours. These tiles imitate the style very effectively, making use of ceramic paints on crisp, white ceramic tiles. Read the manufacturer's instructions for the ceramic paints before you start, especially baking times and temperatures. The tiles can be wiped clean, but don't use harsh abrasives.

YOU WILL NEED

MATERIALS
4 white square ceramic tiles
ceramic paints: dark blue,
  yellow and red

EQUIPMENT
pencil
tracing paper
fine paintbrushes
paint-mixing container

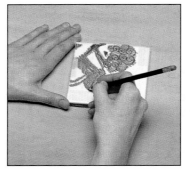

1 Trace the template from the back of the book. Enlarge it on to tracing paper. Transfer a quarter of the design to each tile.

2 With a fine brush and dark blue paint, paint over the main outline on each tile. Heat them in the oven for the specified time, to fix the outline.

3 Fill in the wings, hair and drapery with yellow. Allow the colour to dry. Mix the colours to add darker tones, using the finished picture as a guide. Bake the tiles again, to prevent the colours from smudging.

4 With diluted blue paint, mark in the shadows on the cupid's face and body. Go over any areas that need to be defined with more blue paint. Paint the corner motifs freehand and then bake for the final time.

GINGERBREAD CUPIDS

What better token of your affection than a gift of these gilded cherubs? They are as delicious as they are decorative and would make excellent Christmas-tree hangings.

YOU WILL NEED

MATERIALS
350 g/12 oz/3 cups plain
  white flour
15 ml/1 tbsp ground ginger
7.5 ml/½ tbsp ground cinnamon
2.5 ml/½ tsp grated nutmeg
75 g/3 oz/6 tbsp butter, cut into
  small pieces
50 g/2 oz/4 tbsp soft
  brown sugar
225 g/8 oz/1 cup black treacle
powdered edible food colouring:
  silver and gold

EQUIPMENT
mixing bowl
wooden spoon
baking parchment
rolling pin
pencil
scissors
craft knife
baking sheet
saucer
spoon
fine paintbrush

TO MAKE THE DOUGH:
Sieve the flour and spices into a mixing bowl. Add the butter and rub it in with your fingers, until the mixture looks like fine breadcrumbs. Stir in the sugar. Make a well in the centre and pour in the treacle. Mix well and beat until the mixture comes away from the sides of the bowl. Knead until smooth.

1 Place the dough between two sheets of baking parchment and roll out until very thin. Trace the templates from the back of the book on to baking parchment, cut out and place on the dough. Cut round with the craft knife. Join the sections and mark on details. Place on a baking sheet lined with baking parchment and bake at 180°C/350°F/Gas 4. Leave to cool.

2 Mix the food colouring with water, to make a paste. The easiest way is to tip some on to a saucer, add a drop of water and grind into a paste with the bowl of a spoon. Paint the wings and the centre of the arrows silver.

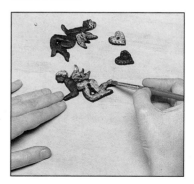

3 Paint the body, the hearts and the flights of the arrows with gold paste. Leave to dry.

GILDED FILIGREE LAMPSHADE

The delicate laciness of filigree work inspired the elegant design for this lampshade. The success depends on arranging cut-out motifs pleasingly, so keep an eye out for decorative paper with suitable designs. You need two papers, one of a lighter weight than the other, such as tissue paper and wrapping paper..

YOU WILL NEED

MATERIALS
cupid-patterned wrapping paper
gold-patterned tissue paper
PVA glue
lampshade
gold acrylic paint

EQUIPMENT
medium and fine paintbrushes
clean cloth (optional)
paint-mixing container

1 Carefully tear around the cupid shapes in the wrapping paper. Tear smaller areas from the gold-patterned tissue paper, for contrast.

3 When dry, decorate the edge of the shade with gold paint.

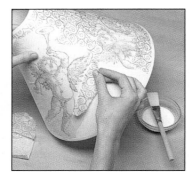

2 Mix equal parts PVA glue and water. Coat the lampshade with this to seal it. Then paint the PVA on to the reverse of the cupid shapes and stick them around the shade. The glue may stretch the paper, so smooth out any wrinkles with a clean cloth (or leave them for added texture). Fill in the areas that are left with the gold-patterned paper, overlapping to make sure the shade is completely covered. Finally, seal the paper with more diluted PVA glue.

CRACKLE-GLAZED "ANTIQUE" PRINT

Antique prints are expensive, but with this technique you can create your own completely original design very cheaply. Use a photocopier to enlarge or reduce motifs and practise arranging them until you have a design that appeals.

YOU WILL NEED

MATERIALS
selection of black and white
  cupid prints
spray adhesive
tea bags and instant coffee
PVA glue
hardboard or cardboard
acrylic medium
clear acrylic gloss varnish
burnt umber acrylic paint

EQUIPMENT
scissors
large soft Chinese paintbrush
household and fine paintbrushes
paint-mixing container

1 Cut out the prints and lightly coat them on the back with spray adhesive. Arrange the prints until you are happy with the result. The advantage of using spray adhesive is that you can reposition them as many times as you like. Photocopy the final result.

2 Make a "cocktail" of one tea bag and three teaspoons of coffee and let it cool. Apply to the print with a Chinese paintbrush. You can experiment with brews of different strengths and apply the mixture several times, to create some depth. Let it dry completely.

3 Mix equal parts PVA glue and water and apply the mixture to the back of the print with a household paintbrush. Smooth the print on to the hardboard or cardboard backing. (You can also apply the print directly to a wall or a piece of furniture.) Brush the PVA mixture on top of the print and backing and leave to dry.

4 Cover the print and backing with acrylic medium in the same way. This may cause the paper to wrinkle, but don't worry: once dry, the wrinkles will vanish.

5 Coat with acrylic varnish, to give a shiny finish and add an antique look.

6 Mix burnt umber acrylic paint into the varnish and paint cracks with a fine paintbrush. Add more shadows and blend them in softly. Finally, apply another coat of acrylic varnish and leave to dry.

CONTEMPLATIVE CUPID CARD

This elaborate hand-made card isn't difficult to make and will tell someone special that they are in your thoughts. Some ordinary pencils are water-soluble, so try what you have before buying pencils specially!

YOU WILL NEED

MATERIALS
heavy watercolour paper
thin card
water-soluble pencils:
  dark green, light green,
  dark blue, light blue, red,
  pink and grey
watercolour or drawing ink:
  pink and orange
all-purpose glue
glitter glue

EQUIPMENT
masking tape
pencil
self-healing cutting mat
craft knife
scissors
fine paintbrush

1 Trace the templates for the background and cupid from the back of the book and enlarge them, if necessary. Tape them to the watercolour paper and go over the outlines with the pencil, leaving an indentation on the paper. Fold along the fold lines.

2 Transfer the design for the frame on to the thin card in the same way. Cut out the card and frame and fold them.

3 Colour in the background and cupid, using the water-soluble pencils, and cut out the cupid. On spare pieces of watercolour paper, draw and colour in some simple flowers and stems. Go over the pencil work with a wet paintbrush, to blend the colours.

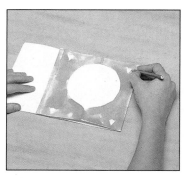

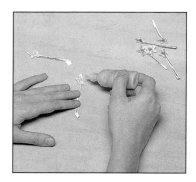

4 Decorate the outside of the card with watercolour or ink, mixing the colours for a patchy effect.

5 Cut out the flowers, stick them together and apply a little glitter glue on to the centres. Apply glitter glue to the wings of the cupid.

6 Line up the edges of the cupid with the edges of the background at points A and C. Stick on some flowers.

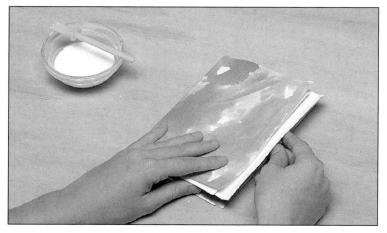

7 Stick the frame to the front of the card at point D. Attach a few more flowers to the inside of the frame.

8 Finally, stick the background and cupid into the card, taking care to line up points B. Stick flap A to join the card together and fold up the card. Press it under a book before sending.

FROSTED GLASS JUG

If you love the effect of frosted glass but don't like the rather banal designs often found in shops, this technique for etching glass, using etching fluid cream, is for you. Why not use the same technique to make a set of glasses to go with the jug, or pick decorative motifs from wallpaper and soft furnishings to make matching glassware?

YOU WILL NEED

MATERIALS
glass jug
etching fluid cream

EQUIPMENT
pencil
scrap paper
scissors
sticky-backed plastic
soft paintbrush
rubber gloves

1 Wash and dry the jug. Draw a cupid and star freehand on to paper and cut out. Trace around the shapes on to sticky-backed plastic and cut out.

2 Peel the backing off the plastic and stick the shapes around the jug.

3 Follow the manufacturer's instructions to paint the etching fluid cream on to the outside of the jug, avoiding the handle. Leave to stand for about 10 minutes.

4 Wearing rubber gloves, wash the cream off the jug in warm water and leave it to dry. If there are any unfrosted patches on the glass where the cream hasn't taken, simply repeat step 3. When you are satisfied with the frosted finish, peel off the shapes.

LOVE-TOKEN BOWL

This bowl is made using a very simple technique but the decorative finish adds a special touch. It would make a delightful container for a Valentine's gift, such as chocolates or a small trinket.

YOU WILL NEED

MATERIALS
petroleum jelly
newspaper
papier-mâché pulp
PVA glue
white acrylic primer
gouache or acrylic paints: blue,
  white, red, yellow and gold
clear gloss varnish

EQUIPMENT
bowl, as a mould
masking tape
medium and fine paintbrushes
paint-mixing container
scissors

1 Line the bowl with petroleum jelly, then newspaper strips. Press a layer of papier-mâché pulp into the bowl. When dry, release from the bowl. Cover the pulp with newspaper strips, dipped in PVA glue.

2 When dry, cover with white primer. Trace the template from the back of the book, enlarging it as required. Snip the edges so the template may be taped flat inside the bowl, and transfer the outline.

3 Paint the background pale blue, dabbing on lighter shades, for a mottled effect.

4 Paint the design, mixing the colours to achieve subtle shades. Paint the rim gold. When dry, give the bowl a coat of varnish.

GILDED CUPID BORDER

This simple version of stencilling produces an extremely effective and eye-catching border. Buy a cheap roll of wallpaper border paper and use the wrong side, then stick the completed design in place. This gets over the problem of stencilling on to a vertical surface.

YOU WILL NEED

MATERIALS
wallpaper border paper
paper glue
aerosol gloss paint
emulsion paint: warm blue and white
silver acrylic paint
rub-on gold paint

EQUIPMENT
stencil card
self-healing cutting mat or cardboard
craft knife
scissors
tracing paper
medium paintbrush
paint-mixing container
masking tape
sponges

1 Trace the template from the back of the book and enlarge it, if necessary. Using a few dabs of glue, stick the template to the stencil card.

2 On a cutting mat or piece of cardboard and using a sharp craft knife, cut out the stencil. Remove the template.

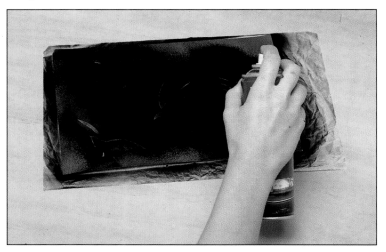

3 Spray both sides of the stencil with gloss paint.

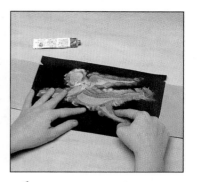

4 In order to line up the design on the border, cut a strip of tracing paper to the width of the border paper. Trace the cupid design on to it, placing it centrally. Place this tracing over the stencil, lining up the cupids. Mark the edges of the stencil at the edges of the tracing paper. Cut notches in the stencil to mark the top and bottom edges of the border. Use these to line up the stencil on the border paper.

5 Paint a background colour of warm blue emulsion on the border paper. Place the stencil over the border, lining up the notches with the top and bottom, and fix it in place with masking tape. Dip a sponge into the silver paint and apply sparingly over the whole stencil. Allow to dry. Repeat along the length of the border. You can use the stencil several times before it becomes clogged, then you will have to cut a new one.

6 Use your finger to apply the gold paint to give depth to the body.

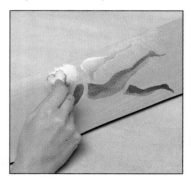

7 Remove the stencil and sponge on the cupids' hair.

▶

8 Apply the doves randomly between the cupids, using white emulsion and a second sponge.

BAROQUE VELVET CUSHION

Use richly coloured velvets and gold braid to create a gorgeous baroque cushion.

YOU WILL NEED

MATERIALS
2 coloured-paper cupid motifs
30 x 40 cm/12 x 16 in
  white cotton fabric
image transfer fluid
fabric glue
42 x 62 cm/16½ x 25 in
  blue velvet
metallic machine embroidery
  threads: gold and red
red velvet scraps
40 cm/16 in gold braid,
  1 cm/½ in wide
2 pearl-drop beads
50 cm/20 in gold cord
matching sewing threads
2 squares matching taffeta,
  42 x 42 cm/16½ x 16½ in
2 m/2 yd wire-edged red
  ribbon, 3 cm/1¼ in wide
40 x 60 cm/16 x 24 in
  cushion pad

EQUIPMENT
dressmaker's scissors
sewing machine
needle

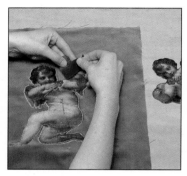

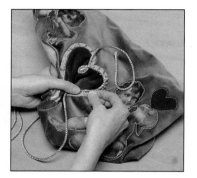

1 Following the manufacturer's instructions, transfer the cupid motifs on to the cotton fabric with image transfer fluid. Cut out each cupid and glue in place on the velvet. Machine-stitch the edges with zigzag stitch using gold thread. Cut one large and two small hearts from the red velvet. Stitch as before, using red metallic thread.

2 Stitch gold braid around the larger heart. Sew a pearl-drop bead to the top and bottom of the heart and trim with gold cord, looping it around the beads. Stitch the cord in place.

3 Make the backing for the cushion with the two squares of taffeta, as described in the Nursery Cushion project. Clip the corners and turn the work the right way out. Cut the wire-edged ribbon into four equal lengths and tie them into bows. Trim the ends to V-shapes and stitch one to each corner. Insert the cushion pad.

CUPID WRAPPING PAPER

This delightful wrapping paper design, with its dropped-shadow image, can be achieved by stencilling or stamping. Home-made wrapping paper would be the perfect finishing touch for a Valentine's Day present or even for a Christmas present; choose appropriate colours for the occasion.

YOU WILL NEED

MATERIALS
plain wrapping paper
acrylic paints: red-oxide
  and gold

EQUIPMENT
cupid motif
acetate sheet
permanent black pen
craft knife
self-healing cutting mat
stencil brush
tile
paint roller
cupid rubber stamp

1 If you are using the stencil method, place a cupid motif (or a freehand sketch) under a sheet of acetate. Draw the image on the acetate with a permanent black pen. Cut it out with the craft knife to create the stencil.

2 Stencil the cupid on to the wrapping paper, using red-oxide paint and a stencil brush. Leave to dry. Using gold paint, stencil the cupid slightly off-centre, for a dropped-shadow effect.

3 If you are using the rubber stamp method, put some red-oxide paint on to the tile and use the roller to coat the stamp. Stamp the images, then over-print using the stamp and the gold paint as before.

CUPID CAMISOLE

This beautiful camisole will make you feel like a million dollars. You will need a commercial paper pattern for a camisole, which is then embellished with machine embroidery. You can embroider over the tissue-paper pattern first and then tear away the paper, leaving an outline to be filled in with colour.

YOU WILL NEED

MATERIALS
*1 m x 90 cm/1 yd x 1 yd
  satin fabric
machine embroidery threads:
  cream, white, gold and grey*

EQUIPMENT
*commercial camisole pattern
dressmaker's scissors
tissue paper
dressmaker's pins
embroidery hoop
sewing machine, with
  darning foot*

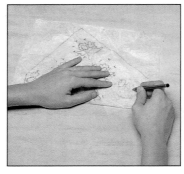

1 Cut out the pattern pieces from the satin, with 1 cm/½ in larger all around, to allow for shrinkage during embroidery. Make a tissue-paper duplicate of the front pattern piece. Trace the template from the back of the book and enlarge it, if necessary. Trace it on to the tissue-paper duplicate, rotating it each time and avoiding the darts.

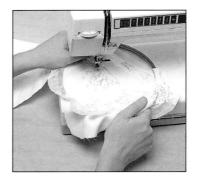

2 Use the tissue duplicate for the embroidering by pinning it to the satin. Place the satin in the embroidery hoop. Set the machine to darning mode and attach the darning foot. With cream thread, stitch the outline of the design.

3 Remove the tissue and fill in the design. Use white thread for the face, body and hearts, gold for the hair and features and grey for the wings and cloud. Make up the camisole according to the pattern instructions.

CUPID DRESSING-TABLE MIRROR

This beautiful dressing-table mirror is made of papier-mâché pulp. Give free rein to your imagination and creativity by hand-painting it in the brightest and most beautiful colours.

YOU WILL NEED

MATERIALS
corrugated cardboard
round mirror, 8 cm/3 in
  diameter
epoxy resin glue
papier-mâché pulp
newspaper
wallpaper paste
PVA glue
white acrylic primer
selection of gouache paints
clear gloss varnish
clear matt varnish
gold enamel paint

EQUIPMENT
pencil
craft knife
self-healing cutting mat
medium, small and fine
  paintbrushes
paint-mixing container

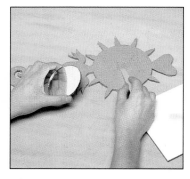

1 Draw your design on to the corrugated cardboard. Cut it out carefully with a sharp craft knife using a cutting mat to protect the work surface.

2 Glue the mirror in position with epoxy resin glue.

3 Carefully build up papier-mâché pulp on the cardboard all around the mirror. Do not place any pulp over the mirror, but ensure the pulp butts up to the edge. Leave to dry thoroughly.

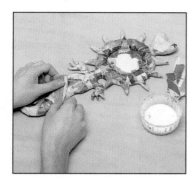

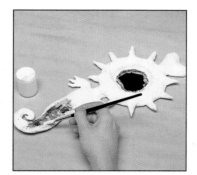

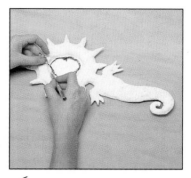

4 Apply several layers of newspaper dipped in wallpaper paste over the dried pulp, just overlapping the edges of the mirror. Allow to dry.

5 Coat with a layer of PVA glue and then white acrylic primer. Allow to dry between each stage.

6 When the paint is dry, cut away the excess paper that overlaps the edge of the mirror, to create a neat finish.

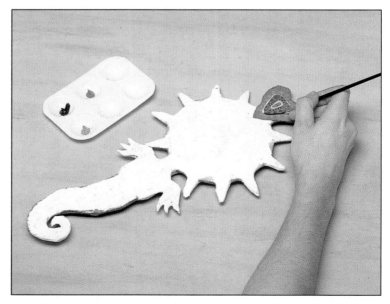

7 Paint on your design in gouache paints, remembering that the back of the mirror is as important as the front.

8 When dry, coat in three or four layers of gloss varnish, adding matt varnish as a contrast in some areas. Allow to dry between each stage. Finish with gold enamel detail.

FOLK-ART STYLE HAND-PAINTED BOX

The cupid motif is popular in traditional folk-art designs. Here it has been used to embellish an oval Shaker-style box. The distressed hand-painted finish gives it a timeless quality that will ensure it is treasured for ever.

YOU WILL NEED

MATERIALS
oval cardboard box
corrugated cardboard
white glue
newspaper
wallpaper paste
white acrylic primer
acrylic paints: dark green,
  brick red, yellow ochre,
  pale blue and brown

EQUIPMENT
craft knife
self-healing cutting mat
medium and fine paintbrushes
paint-mixing container
sandpaper

1 Trace the templates from the back of the book, enlarging them to fit the lid of your box. Trace the shapes onto the corrugated cardboard. Cut them out and glue them to the lid of the box with white glue.

2 Soak small strips of newspaper in the wallpaper paste. Stick three layers over the edges of the cardboard shapes. Allow to dry. Paint the lid and box with white acrylic primer.

3 Paint the box and the background of the lid dark green. When dry, paint with brick red. When dry, sand down for a distressed finish.

4 Paint the cupid, mixing the colours to create subtle shades. Use a fine brush for the border and the decoration. Stipple the cheeks with a dry brush.

CUPID LINOCUT

Linocut images have a pleasing graphic simplicity. Here the marvellous texture and light-enhancing qualities of gold metallic organza are contrasted with the solidity of the image. The beauty of linocuts is that the lino block can be used lots of times, so this idea can be adapted for making, for example, your own Christmas cards.

YOU WILL NEED

MATERIALS
printing inks: red and blue
gold metallic organza
decorative paper
picture frame

EQUIPMENT
lino block
lino-cutting tools: U-shaped
  scoop and V-shaped nib
plate
paint roller
masking tape
scrap paper

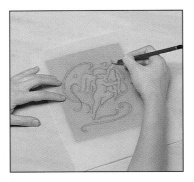

1 Trace the template from the back of the book and transfer the design to the lino block. Cut the design with the cutting tools: use the scoop to cut out large background areas and the nib for fine details.

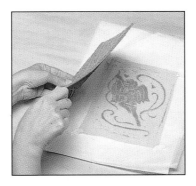

2 Squeeze the printing inks on to the plate and use the roller to mix the colours to get a deep burgundy shade. Coat the roller evenly, then roll over the surface of the lino cut.

3 Tape the corners of the metallic organza to the scrap paper to ensure the fabric is wrinkle free. Position the linocut over the organza and press evenly to ensure a crisp, solid print. Use the decorative paper to create a mount for the picture, then frame.

WINGS OF LOVE WALL DECORATION

Salt-dough is a marvellous medium for making three-dimensional decorations. This wall decoration could also be incorporated into a Christmas decoration scheme.

YOU WILL NEED

MATERIALS
200 g/7 oz/1 cup salt
250 g/8 oz/2 cups flour
paper clip
white acrylic primer
acrylic paints: verdigris
  and bronze

EQUIPMENT
mixing bowl
spoon
baking parchment
modelling tools
flat pliers
scissors
medium and fine paintbrushes
small sponge

TO MAKE THE SALT DOUGH:
Put the salt and flour in a large bowl. Gradually pour in cold water and stir until the mixture forms a dough. Remove from the bowl and knead on a floured surface for 10 minutes.

1 Trace the template from the back of the book and enlarge it on to baking parchment. For the outer wings, make 10 thin rolls of dough. Moisten the edges and press gently together on the template. Use a flat-edged modelling tool to make "feathers".

2 Shape the inner wing to fit the baking parchment outline. Moisten the back of the wing and press it gently into place. Make the face and hair in the same way, shaping the pieces separately and pressing them into place. Cut the paper clip in half with the pliers. Press one piece into the top of the cupid's head for hanging.

3 Bake for at least eight hours at the lowest setting on your oven. The dough is cooked when it sounds hollow when tapped. Trim the baking parchment. Allow to cool. Leaving to dry between each stage, paint with white acrylic primer, then the verdigris paint. Finally burnish the raised details with bronze paint.

"IVORY" CUPID

Plaster blanks are now readily available, and can be customized with the paint finish of your choice. Here, the plaster has been given an antique ivory finish, but you could experiment with distressed metallic effects, such as gold or verdigris.

YOU WILL NEED

MATERIALS
shellac sanding sealer
plaster cupid
raw umber emulsion paint

EQUIPMENT
medium paintbrushes
paint-mixing container
kitchen paper or soft cloth

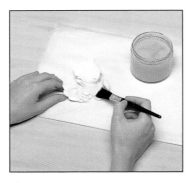

1 Paint shellac sanding sealer all over the cupid, using a medium paintbrush. Leave the sealer to dry for half an hour, then apply another coat, and leave to dry again.

2 Dilute the raw umber emulsion paint with water, until it is the consistency of double cream. Paint the watered-down emulsion all over the cupid.

3 While the paint is still wet, rub it off using kitchen paper or a soft cloth, so that the paint only remains in the crevices. Be sure to use a clean spot each time you rub, or you will put the paint back on.

GOLD AND SILVER VALENTINE'S CARD

A handmade Valentine's card really conveys your feelings. This card captures the spirit of elaborate Victorian Valentine's cards, with its combination of gold and silver lace, soft, velvety pink background and central cupid motif. Yet it is very easy to make using paper doilies, which instantly give a delicate, antique look.

YOU WILL NEED

MATERIALS
paper glue
15 cm/6 in square dark pink
  paper
20 cm/8 in square gold card
decorative gold cake band
silver, white and gold
  paper doilies
lilac and dark green paper
  scraps
Victorian-style cupid motif

EQUIPMENT
scissors

1 Glue the pink paper to the gold card, leaving an equal margin all around. Trim the edges with narrow strips of gold foil lace, cut from the cake band. Cut out a small silver flower for each corner from the silver doilies.

2 Cut out four white petals and two flower shapes from a white doily and back them with lilac paper. Choose a larger rectangular shape for the centre and back it with dark green paper. Stick the backed shapes on to the background.

3 Cut out silver flowers and white leaves and glue them around the edges of the main shape, in an interesting pattern.

4 Finish by fixing the cupid to the centre and adding more cut-out gold flowers.

TEMPLATES

To enlarge the templates to the correct size, use either a grid system or a photocopier. For the grid system, trace the template and draw a grid of evenly spaced squares over your tracing. To scale up, draw a larger grid on to another piece of paper. Copy the outline on to the second grid by taking each square individually and drawing the relevant part of the outline in the larger square. Finally, draw over the lines to make sure they are continuous.

Cupid Camisole p44

Majolica-style Tiles p20

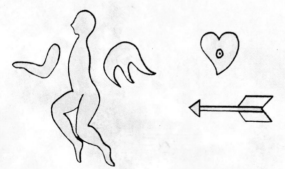

Gingerbread Cupids p22

Wings of Love Wall Decoration p54

Folk-art Style Hand-painted Box p50

Winged Cupid Brooch p14

Gilded Cupid Border p36

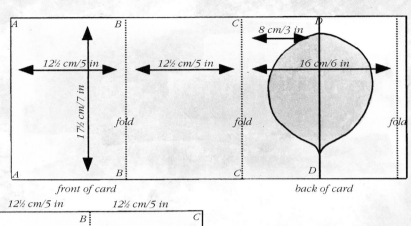

front of card

back of card

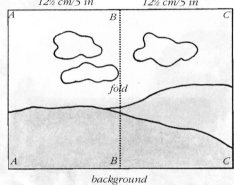

background

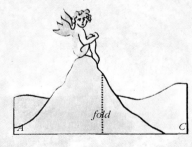

Contemplative Cupid Card p. 29

Nursery Cushion with Musical Cupid p12

Love-token Bowl p34

Cupid Linocut p52

ACKNOWLEDGEMENTS

The author and publishers would like to thank the following people for designing the projects in this book:

Ofer Acoo

Copper Cupid Mobile pp16–19; Crackle-glazed "Antique" Print pp27–28

Madeleine Adams

Love-token Bowl pp34–35

Petra Boase

Frosted Glass Jug pp32–33

Louise Brownlow

Gingerbread Cupids pp22–23; Contemplative Cupid Card pp29–31; Gilded Cupid Border pp36–39

Lucinda Ganderton

Nursery Cushion with Musical Cupid pp12–13; Majolica-style Tiles pp20–21; Baroque Velvet Cushion pp40–41; Folk-art Style Hand-painted Box pp50–51; Wings of Love Wall Decoration pp54–55; Gold and Silver Valentine's Card pp58–59

Stephanie Harvey

"Ivory" Cupid pp56–57;

Kim Rowley

Winged Cupid Brooch pp14–15; Cupid Dressing-table Mirror pp46–49

Isabel Stanley

Cupid Camisole pp44–45

Josephine Whitfield

Gilded Filigree Lampshade pp24–25; Cupid Wrapping Paper pp42–43

Picture Credits
Bridgeman Art Library/Fitzwilliam Museum, University of Cambridge: p8 bottom; Bridgeman Art Library/Richard Philp: p9 top; Bridgeman Art Library p11 right; ET Archive p8 top; p9 bottom; p10; Visual Arts Library p11 bottom.